MW01102643

A Husky Howls

by

Denny-in-the-Wind

authorHOUSE™

1663 LIBERTY DRIVE, SUITE 200
BLOOMINGTON, INDIANA 47403
(800) 839-8640
WWW.AUTHORHOUSE.COM

First published by AuthorHouse 10/08/04

ISBN: 1-4208-0250-X (e)
ISBN: 1-4208-0249-6 (sc)

Library of Congress Control Number: 2004098123

Printed in the United States of America
Bloomington, Indiana

This book is printed on acid-free paper.

Special Acknowledgments

I wish to give special Thanks to Brian Crowder for the many hours of editing Denny's book. His wife Liz who was a good friend and like a sister to Denny helped me with the pictures and was on the phone to me almost every day keeping me focused. Our parents Al and Grace helped with pictures and the summary in the back of this book about the Author. Also last but for sure not least Drew Starr & Mike Lansell whom have been so supportive to my parents and myself, Debbie. I know Denny is smiling to see his life long friends and family able work together and get his work published. Brian & Liz of Texas, myself in Washington and Drew, Mike and my Parents in Ohio the miles were not a barrier. Also I would like the many friends that helped and were there for Denny as he was there for many of them, each having a different story.

Dedication

For Currumpaw's Ice Dancer who stayed by me through difficult times, and through her love for me that poured from her eyes. I remembered and wrote her story for all to know so that the Currumpaw pack will live on through the joy a reader may find in this book.

To the Chukchi and their sled dogs: For Togo, the greatest of all lead dogs; for the relay mushers of the Nome serum drive and all the huskies from that drive which the native people call "The Great Race of Mercy" that this book will bring back to the modern world that which should not be lost:

In order of the mushers' relay to Nome:

- "Wild Bill" Shannon - 52 miles
- Edgar Kalland – 52 miles
- Dan Green – 28 miles
- Johnny Folger – 26 miles
- Sam Joseph – 34 miles
- Titus Nikolai – 24 miles
- Dave Corning – 30 miles
- Harry Pitka – 30 miles
- Bill McCarty – 28 miles
- Edgar Nollner - 24 miles (Athabascan Indian)
- George Nollner – (Athabascan Indian)
- Charlie Evans – 30 miles
- Tommy Patsy – 36 miles
- Jackscrew – 40 miles (Koyukuk Indian)
- Victor Anagick – 34 miles (Inuit native American Eskimo)
- Myles Gonangan – 40 miles
- Henry Ivanoff – (Chukchi native Siberian living in Alaska)
- **Leonard Seppala—and Togo - 340 miles**
- Charlie Olsen – 25 miles
- Gunnar Kaasen—and Balto – 53 miles

Table of Contents

Preface

This is the story of the Currumpaw Siberian sled dogs. Covering the history of how a tribe of the Chukchi brought them to America. The Chukchi, also known by the name of their larger tribes, the [Luoravetlan] Lygoraveltlat, were the people who lived in the Northeast of Siberia.

The story of a musher from the 1920's named Leonard Seppalla and the great serum run which saved the lives of many children.

The complete story told by Denny current day musher and the history and personality of each dog's role in the pack and on the sled.

"This simple story is a part of the most precious experiences I have ever had, one that few in the modern world will ever experience. While reading this, please keep in mind that this is not a sad story, but a joyous story. A story about a link to the past and a wonderful experience, about love and togetherness, the cycle of life and the indomitable spirit of the sled dog."

Endurance – Fidelity -- Intelligence

Mush

This is the story of the Currumpaw Siberians. The Currumpaw Siberian sled dogs were named after the Currumpaw wolf and his mate, Blanca[1]. The true story of the Currumpaw Wolf is about strong and undying love as wolves mate for life, and hidden in its text is a message about the strength of the female and that the male and female of any species compliment each other physically and spiritually.

For years I would tell people stories about the Currumpaws, and they told me that I should write this book. A nice thought, but I didn't think it was something that people wanted to read about. In this modern age of movies, computers and technology, anything seems possible, and this story is a simple one and perhaps such things were no longer meant to be known. The story of the Currumpaws was locked into my memories, and had special meaning to me. It would be difficult to write about it in a way that people would enjoy, it would be difficult for me to put so much time and effort into writing something that may not be appreciated.

My feelings on this changed thanks to one sled dog, Blanca. Blanca used to sit outside and let out long, awful and mournful howls. Blanca was surely the happiest dog ever, but these sad howls went on every day. Her howls were loud, long, and constantly changing but always seemed to carry a message of sadness.

Blanca's howls rang through the huskies' land each day. I believe that there are many reasons she let out these howls, but surely one of the reasons was mourning the passing of what once was — days when the sled dog had a special place in the world, days when they served the thing they loved the most—"the People". Progress and technology have moved society beyond the need for the sled dog. I used to talk to my sled dogs and would tease them about this because it was something they didn't know. In their minds, they served me, and they believed that mushing, the thing they loved to do was necessary to me. This feeling never left me.

One night as I stood outside and listened to Blanca's sad songs, and somehow as if she were communicating it to me, I realized she was telling me that there was a story to tell.

Though this is the story of the Currumpaw sled dogs, it has a deeper meaning as well - that God sends us our people and gives us the Earth and we must not turn our back on those gifts for in doing so we would be turning our back on God. It tells us too that when love and goodness comes from within you will be blessed; that love will cause the shift to good from that which is dark and would destroy us.

This simple story is part of one of the most precious experiences I have ever had, one that few in the modern world will ever experience. All the events in this story are true; the thoughts that I write about, I actually had at the time. While reading this, please keep in mind that this is not a sad story, but a joyous story. A story about a link to the past and a wonderful experience, about love and togetherness, the cycle of life, and the indomitable spirit of the sled dog as described on a statue of the heroic lead dog Balto in Central Park which forever honors them:

"Endurance—Fidelity—Intelligence"

That Which Makes the Chukchi Dog's Spirit Strong

The native people call the sled dogs "spirit dogs". The Chukchi bred their little dogs for over three thousand years and considered them nearly equal to any member of their tribe.

All the Siberian Huskies we see today came from the original Chukchi seventy-five as a result of the centuries-long wars between Russia and the Chukchi. During these wars, the Russians would often force the dog-breeding culture Chukchi into retreat until the Chukchi had no choice but to enter the water on their little boats and take their chances with their other enemy - the kayak culture Inuit, the American Eskimos.

Each Chukchi family would put their best dogs into the small boats. With so little room on the boats, they would kill the rest of the dogs and even some of their own children in favor of the sled dog - the foundation of their culture and their means of survival. This has made the spirit of the sled dog strong with the Earth (God). The Russians exterminated all the Chukchi's dogs shortly after the seventy-five came to Alaska.

The Chukchi say that there was a day long ago when the numbers of the tribe and the sled dogs were decimated by famine. Finally the last two remaining pups were nursed at a woman's breast to insure the survival of the breed.

Innisfree and the Chukchi Sled Dog

Innisfree is the most highly regarded Siberian Husky kennel. Kathleen Kanzler, the kennel owner, breeds the finest Siberian Husky show dogs in the world. One of her dogs even won Best in Show at the most prestigious dog show of all, the Westminster Kennel Club show in New York City. The standard to which Siberian Huskies are bred and shown is considered a benchmark in the breeding world. A wise and experienced breeder, Kathleen knew that it would be best for the breed to integrate the Siberian Husky's most distinct and important attribute, the ability to work as part of a sled team, into her breeding program.

The Siberian Huskies were originally bred by a people who lived in the Northeast of Siberia, the Chukchi. They were also known by the name of one of their larger tribes, the [Luoravetlan] Lygoraveltlat. They were people native to the land and over the centuries had territorial wars with the other native people in the region, the Samoyeds, who lived to the south, and the Inuit, who lived across the water in the land now called Alaska. The wars left the Chukchi living in the most barren part of the tundra. The barren land with its harsh weather left the Chukchi with little food.

To survive, the Chukchi started breeding dogs to pull sleds with which they could travel hundreds of miles to hunt and gather. They became a dog breeding culture with each generation of young dogs better than the last. This went on for three thousand years and, according to experts, makes the Chukchi dogs the most pure of the pure bred dogs. The result was a small, strong, energy-conserving dog possessing great endurance and the ability to withstand the harsh cold. The Chukchi dogs required very little food, could run fast, and could pull heavy loads for hundreds of miles. They were covered in arctic fur with sturdy guard hairs that shed water and snow, keeping them warm and dry. When the temperature dropped to fifty below zero, the little dogs slept warm and comfortable and would sleep in a little ball with their thick furry tails wrapped around their face.

The Chukchi would also let their dogs sleep in their houses, huddled in their beds to help keep them warm. Legend has it that temperatures at night were measured in terms of the number of dogs necessary to stay warm, giving rise to the expressions "two dog night and three dog night". The huskies were also companion dogs for the Chukchi children, who would learn about the nature and instincts of the dogs. These skills aided the children when they reached adulthood. Managing the dog teams was crucial to the survival of the tribe.

The Chukchi dogs came in many colors and had many different types of markings. Many had blue eyes, and some had one blue eye and one brown eye. Some huskies had great big spots or asymmetrical markings on their faces. Others still carried the markings of the king of the arctic, their near ancestors of the same species, Canis Lupus, the wolf. The Alaskans at the time of the gold rush often referred to the Chukchi dogs as Siberian Wolf Dogs. The wolfish markings became the favorite of breeders and today the Siberian Huskies are typified by that look.

Siberians basically come in two colors, red and black. Both color dogs have white undersides and white snouts. If the guard hairs are solid in color, the dogs will have a rich color, such as black. If the guard hairs are tipped in color, then black becomes grey, and red becomes light red. Although many Siberians that are bought as pets are black and white, often with matching blue eyes, the breeders of today do not focus on these colors, or even eye color. Most of the Currumpaw Siberians were light red with eyes that were brownish red and which matched their lips, nose, and the skin around their eyes. Many people thought that they were young wolves because of the light red color of their fur.

For the Chukchi sled dog, life in the village was seasonal. Every spring the people would let the sled dogs loose, and the dogs would fend for themselves and hunt in packs. To control breeding and the progress of their breeding program; the lead dogs and their breeding stock were kept in the villages year round. All other males were neutered. By being allowed to hunt until these most recent times, there is a wildness instilled in the Chukchi dog that is not found in other domesticated dogs. Huskies are predators and have strong instincts for the order of the pack. They have a passion for the moment and a lust for life because, for the predator, there may be no tomorrow. The predator lives well with heartbreak and suffering. The predator has a symbiotic existence with nature.

This symbiotic existence is best exemplified by the Inuit story of how wolves were created:

God looked across his Land and saw the need to create another beautiful thing. He reached into a hole and pulled out the Caribou. The Caribou would run in herds and compliment the beauty and splendor of the Land. But soon the Caribou herd became weak, plagued with sickness. God decided that he must create a cure for the Caribou's weaknesses, so he reached back into the hole and pulled out the wolf. The wolf would keep the Caribou strong by weeding out the sick, and reinforce the safety the Caribou found in the togetherness of the herd.

My Currumpaws

I loved the sled dog and its cousin, the wolf, and believed that if huskies were truly loved and allowed to let their natural instincts of the pack and its social order mature, that I would have a wonderful life with them, and that together they would make an exquisite sled team. To that end a little puppy was put in a plastic crate and by car, train, boat, and airplane, came to me. He was Innisfree's Jim Brandenburg.

After Brandenburg came to me, the girl I had waited for many years arrived. This was special because her sire, Chrisdon's Triple Bogey, or "Duffer", was rarely bred. Duffer's whelps were the smartest and strongest Siberians with a rare, highly-prized, total obedience and attentiveness. This new pup would become the Alpha female, the highest raking female of the pack and my constant companion. She would grow to look at me with a love pouring from her eyes such as I have never seen. She was Currumpaw's Natasha Ko. I would often call her KoKo, or Tasha.

Ko is a legend of sorcery. To escape death from enemies, sorcerers and their mates would stare at Ko, which would transform them from human to wolf allowing them to escape their enemies. They would then live out the rest of their days as arctic wolves. I included the word Ko in the new pup's name out of fascination for the story. Little did I know that this wonderful animal, with her great intelligence, would come to have human qualities deserving of that name. When people would stand around talking, Tasha would struggle to understand the conversation, her head tilting side to side out of frustration at not being able to comprehend every sentence and word. Brandenburg loved Tasha and she loved him. Theirs was a perfect love, a love so rarely seen. I would have envied them if it weren't for the great love they would come to show me. Of course, regarding love, they were Currumpaws.

Following Tasha came Blanca, making the same trip as Brandenburg, hand selected to be a perfect mate for him. Blanca would become the Omega female, the lowest ranking member of the pack, a difficult yet important position, but a position that she loved. I trained the three huskies to pull their sled. At first, I trained Brandenburg to respond to left and right commands, gee and haw. I teamed the three dogs with Brandenburg and Tasha hitched next to each other in the lead positions, and Blanca who alone worked the wheel position closest to the sled. Natasha with her innate desire to respond to my wishes quickly learned the role of the lead dog from Brandenburg. They would compete to see who could respond most quickly to my commands and who could figure out difficult directional changes first. Brandenburg was a great lead dog, always working hard and never stepping in soft or wet snow. Brandenburg had a wonderful ability to lead the small team.

Every Currumpaw Morning

As I was sleeping one morning I was awakened by the most disturbing sound, a loud combination of a whelp, a moan, and a scream. Innisfree's Blanca of Currumpaw (Blanca) water had broken and she was giving birth. I went to see Blanca after she made that horrible sound, and sat with her for many hours. It was first and only time I ever experienced birth. The first to be born was a solid red female. When she grew, she followed me around everywhere, looking up at me with her big brown eyes—she seemed to love me. She was spunky and I called her Stormy. Then came a very white female, light red as we say, but her hind legs came first. She didn't pass easy, but I learned what to do, and eventually grabbed her hind legs and pulled her out. I called her Wrong Way. As Wrong Way grew she became uncommonly dainty and pretty. This wonderful pup soon came to be known as Pretty and, eventually, Ici.

I had to sell most of the puppies, because I didn't really have room for them all. I wanted them to have good homes. Pretty was such an attractive puppy that she was quickly taken home by a pro football player named David who wanted his three year old son to grow up with a nice dog. A few day after I sold the puppy named Pretty, David, her new owner, came to my home and sadly returned the little puppy because his wife didn't want to deal with the mess the baby Siberian might make of their home. That night I went to bed and Pretty crawled into bed with me falling asleep over my right leg. I could never part with her again. Pretty would sleep over my right leg for most of the rest of her life. In hindsight, I believe there were many reasons beyond fate for Pretty's return to me. By coming back Pretty would have the chance to live a life very different from that of a simple, family pet. She would grow to be a sled dog and inhabit a very special place in my life. David had changed Pretty's name to Ice and upon her return I renamed her Ici. She is Currumpaw's Ice Dancer.

Ici is a little, red, female Siberian Husky, but unlike the Siberians we often see proudly walking with their owners, riding in their cars - Ici is a sled dog. Ici's fur is almost pure white, adorned with guard hairs tipped with light red. Like most red Siberians, her lips, nose, and eyelids are a liver color and match her eyes. Ici bears a stunning resemblance to a little lead dog named Togo that lived in the 1920's.

Blanca would have two more puppies that night.

After Pretty came the "monster puppy", distress and horror, it was too big to pass, and Blanca would surely die. But I used all the tricks I learned to help her. After a long time the puppy came out, but it was dead from having its umbilical cord squeezed in the birth canal for so long.

After Blanca delivered the still-born monster puppy, out came another light red girl. This little cinnamon colored girl was behind the monster puppy and was stuck in the birth canal for a long time. She too was limp and lifeless. The little lifeless puppy just covered the palm of my hand. She felt heavy but I thought perhaps it was not too late. I rubbed her heart over and over, and blew into her mouth - seemingly forever. How sad I thought, she was gone - I kept rubbing her heart anyway, blowing air into her mouth, her little lips spreading as the air passed in. Suddenly she came to life! Somewhere in her unconsciousness she fought and fought for life. The little cinnamon girl quickly recovered from her difficult birth and was thriving—she was a survivor.

Later, I realized that this little cinnamon girl must stay. She would grow to be the strongest sled dog I have ever seen. She was protective of me and her pack and lived with a lust for life as no other. The rest of my time with her I would be in awe of her. This feeling never left me. She was Leto, Currumpaw's Leto. Leto's name came from the god-mother of Mercury. Losing favor with Zeus, Leto had lived her life as a wolf to hide from his anger.

After Leto's birth I wrapped the monster puppy in a towel and respectfully laid him in a safe place near the whelping den. I looked at the still, little puppy wrapped in the towel I noticed that his face had that cute look that newborn puppies have, a sort of helpless expression with their eyes closed tight. I thought of the fact that this little one would miss all the pleasures of life, running with other huskies, being loved - love returned from the people he would have loved with all his heart and soul. I realized that the little dog should have a place to rest fit for what he was born to be, a Chukchi sled dog.

After resting, I placed the puppy's body in the dog bag on the sled. I hitched up Brandenburg and Tasha to mush the puppy to a peaceful place far into the woods. We stopped at a location just thirty feet from a beautiful trail that runs along a stream. A trail that my sled dogs would run with a pure joy— they were perfection in motion. I buried the puppy there in this place where my team would occasionally mush by so that even after death perhaps he could feel the joy of what it was to be a Currumpaw.

Before the puppies were born I built a whelping den. A special warm place where the puppies would be born and where Blanca could go in and nurse them. The whelping den was built to keep the puppies in and allow Blanca to leave the den so as to get her much needed space away from them to recover from nursing. Only days after the puppies were born, I would wake in the morning to find Leto out of the puppy den, nursing alone on an annoyed Blanca. Leto was yet unable to walk and Blanca certainly would not pick her up and move her out of the den, so how did she get out? One night I spied on her. Leto crawled up to the dividing board that kept the puppies in, rested, and then pushed her little body up the side like a snake until she could get her little elbows over the top. Exhausted, she rested hanging there by her elbows. Then in one last big effort she would pull herself over the top falling onto the floor with a loud plunk. Then, she would crawl to Blanca and nurse alone the rest of the night. This would be her way for the rest of her life, fighting to run fastest, experience all that the world had to offer, and showing me how precious life was.

During the Serum run to Nome, dogs froze on their feet while mushing—it is this spirit that makes the Chukchi dog strong. Leto would gladly have frozen on her feet, if necessary, to help the lead dog bring the team home.

Leto would power the team in races. They were so fast that in their first major race, a race that is normally decided within seconds between teams that came from across the country, the Currumpaw Siberians won with a lead of over eight minutes. After that year organizers shortened the race distance to help make the other teams more competitive. Still, the Currumpaws won time after time.

Leto was Ici's friend; they were inseparable. They were like Frick and Frack and their ridiculous antics brought many joyous days of laughter and happiness to me. As young puppies they were constantly into things, running, playing with each other, and spending time outside gazing at the wonders of the world. One day the two puppies played so much outside, running and playing wolf tag that they were covered in mud, from head to toe, only the whites of their faces saved from the mud. I laughed and played with them, each of them trying to play wolf tag with me, sneaking up behind me and charging at me trying to knock me over with little body slams until I too was covered in mud. I will always remember them this way.

As Leto matured she became the guard dog, protector of the pack, and would sit high on a sandstone slab on their land or high on a perch in the front of the house and gaze out over her territory. Ici would often lie by her side. As the protector of the pack, there were many instances when Leto fulfilled her role as protector of life. She had a strong instinct that seemed to enable her to tell when someone had ill intentions and there were many instances that she demonstrated this. Among the most memorable stories is an incident which occurred one evening in January just after a light snowfall when an intruder opened a window to enter the house.

Leto would spend her time in her private place under a small table and would actually get up and walk the house at regular intervals to make sure everything was okay. While sleeping under the table, she realized that a window was opening upstairs. She let out a "danger bark", a slightly muffled bark, and bolted toward the stairs. Upon hearing the danger bark the other four huskies followed quickly. The five huskies hurried along after Leto, excited by the prospect of the adventure, and thrilled to move together as a pack. There they were, the five huskies standing together on my bed with Leto at the front snarling and growling. The intruder quickly closed the window; he didn't even have time to try to get through it. What a frightening site it must have been, seeing the five wolf-looking huskies, ready to move in unison against him. The experience made Leto proud and all of the huskies glowed with pride as they descended the stairs, each feeling a great sense of purpose. They returned to their places and rested as if nothing happened.

Leto loved to watch television, especially loving to watch shows with wild animals. As the protector of the pack, she would respond to anything that stimulated any of her senses. Even though the television gave no scent from the animals it displayed, and Leto knowing that they weren't really there, she loved to stare at them, getting excited, and occasionally touching her nose to the tube to make sure there really wasn't an animal in there. Leto would play outside with her mother Blanca for hours. King of the mountain - taunting each other, dropping on their forearms with their butts in the air, woofing, one charging the other, the other running playfully, laughing as only huskies can. Tag, you're it—suddenly the pursuer was the pursued, running and laughing. That's wolf tag, a game played by wolves—and sled dogs.

Sep, Togo, and the All Alaska Sweepstakes

All the Siberian Huskies are descended from an original seventy-five dogs that were brought to Alaska in the 1920's from the Chukchi people in Siberia, who bred them for three thousand years. The Chukchi dog is the Siberian Husky; they were brought over to race in the sweepstakes sled dog races. The Alaskans made millions on the gold rush, but because of the months of travel it took to return to the lower forty-eight states, they had nothing to spend their money on. They used dogs to pull the gold ore out of the mines through tiny tunnels, and used them to pull sleds. They each would brag that their dogs were the best, so they bet on dog sled races. They would pool their riches creating large cash prize lists equal to a million of today's dollars, hence the word sweepstakes. The Chukchi dogs were small, fast, energy conserving sled dogs. They dominated the races. They had many unusual names; one was called Ici.

A musher named Leonhard Seppala came to Alaska and began working as a sled dog caretaker and trainer. "Sep", as he was referred to, began mushing his own teams and became one of the best racers. When the Siberians were first brought to Alaska, Sep became one of the first racers to run them. He began his Siberian Husky breeding program, which included a breeding of his dog Dolly, and his lead dog Suggen. Sep was a man of small stature, which probably gave him some advantage on the trail. Once he began mushing the little Chukchi sled dogs, the mushers often referred to him as "the little man with the little dogs".

The breeding of Dolly and Suggen produced only one puppy, a very small male that Sep called Togo. Togo seemed too small to grow to be a sled dog, and as a young puppy Togo was very mischievous, always taunting or trying to play with the sled dogs. Togo loved Seppala and would follow him everywhere. Sep already had his hands full with his team and this little puppy was plenty of trouble, and he thought Togo was too small to be a sled dog. Being the puppy of a lead dog Togo had some value as a working dog and Sep recognized that the little dog was uncommonly smart. When Togo turned eight weeks old, Sep sold the dog to a local farmer who could raise him to be a farm dog.

Even at this young age, Togo would have none of this farm life and made himself a nuisance. Togo would taunt the pigs, trying

21

to get them to play, which of course they wouldn't. When the farmer would call Togo, the little dog would run away and hide in the woods. Togo would dig holes everywhere, dig up the gardens, and howl all night long keeping the farmers awake. The farmer had enough of the bad little dog and he returned Togo to Seppala.

A woman named Mrs. Robinson lived near Seppala and would visit him often. She absolutely loved the playful little Togo and would bring the puppy treats and shower him with attention. Togo loved life around the sled dogs, but Sep still didn't want to keep the little dog so he gave the young pup to Mrs. Robinson. Togo liked Mrs. Robinson, but he liked life in the dog yard better and would run away every chance he could—right back to Sep's dog yard. Seppala finally gave in and decided to keep the little dog.

One night Seppala was called to duty and hitched up his best team to mush to a neighboring village called Dime Creek, a journey of three days. Sep, knowing how mischievous and smart Togo was, put the little dog in a kennel with high fences where he would be safe until he returned and off Sep went with his team.

Togo did not like being kept in the kennel and howled and cried all day long. Sep had a dog handler watching the dogs that were left back home and he had specifically instructed the handler never to let Togo out - no matter what. The first night Sep was away the handler heard screaming coming from the kennels. Not suspecting that the cries were the sound of the always complaining Togo the handler ran to the kennel. There he found Togo hanging upside down from the top of the fence with his flank caught in the sharp wire. The handler cut Togo off the fence with wire cutters but before he could grab the little dog Togo jumped up and bolted off into the night.

It was now the morning of the second day of Seppala's mush to Dime Creek and Sep hitched the team and took off on the day's journey. Shortly after they started Sep saw a fox on the trail so he stopped the team so the dogs wouldn't be distracted by the fox while on trail. Wildlife most often flee at the sight of a sled team thinking it's a pack of wolves.

Suddenly the fox began to run towards the team and the team began lunging in their harnesses towards the fox. Sep was disturbed by this as he wondered what kind of crazy animal would run toward a sled team. This also frightened Sep because he knew the only solution would be to secure the sled into the snow with an ice hook and get in front of the team and shoot the fox before it reached the team. Suddenly Sep realized that it wasn't a fox after all; it was that damn little dog Togo!

Seppala could not take the time to return Togo and the little dog's injuries hadn't stopped him from picking up the team's scent trail and running to catch up so Sep tended to the little dog's injury and put him in the dog bag on the sled. A dog bag is a special bag in which sled dogs might ride if they injured a paw or pulled a muscle while on the trail. While riding in the bag the husky's head would stick out of the bag allowing the dog to watch the scenery and the sled team. Siberians have strong pack instincts and riding in the dog bag made Togo very unhappy. He should be running with his pack – not sitting in a bag! Togo began to scream and cry. After a while Sep could no longer stand all the annoying noise that the little dog was making, so he relented and hitched Togo to the team.

Watching Togo run with the team for the first time, Sep realized that this dog was all business. Togo was fully concentrating on the run and pulling harder than any of the other dogs. Sep decided to take a chance and move the little dog up to the middle of the team, in a swing position, where it is most important for the dogs to stay right on trail ensuring the team stays in line even when encountering wildlife and other distractions.

Togo kept running perfectly and was working very hard. Sep could tell how hard a dog was working by how much tension the dog kept on the tug line, the line that runs from the back of the harness to the gang line. Sep kept moving him up in the team until finally he hitched Togo next to the lead dog. Togo learned the lead commands immediately and kept his tug line tight on the entire mush. From that day on Togo was a lead dog and soon became Sep's best lead dog. Sep and Togo went on to dominate the All Alaska Sweepstakes and the other great races of Alaska.

Togo's Run: "The Great Race of Mercy"

On January 20, 1925 a telegraph message was sent from Nome, "Nome calling...Nome calling...We have an outbreak of diphtheria...No serum...Urgently need help...Nome calling... Nome calling..." There was a diphtheria epidemic in Nome in the middle of Alaska's harsh winter.

Serum was too far away, over a thousand miles away in Anchorage. Heavy snow was falling and the weather conditions were far beyond that which the airplanes of the time could handle with their open cockpits. In fact, it was so cold that the engines of the available aircraft were frozen and would not start. The city would die - all the children would surely die.

A telegraph message was sent to Nome, "Anchorage calling... Anchorage calling...300,000 units of serum located in railway hospital here...Package can be shipped by train to Nenana - package weighs 20 pounds...Could serum be carried to Nome on Iditarod trail by mail drivers and dog teams?"

Mail was usually carried by dogsled along the Iditarod trail and it was believed that they could run the relay by assembling the sled dog teams at fifty-mile intervals and rush the serum to

Nome. Leonard Seppala raced the best of the Chukchi dogs. Only fifty miles from Nome, he mushed his team, with the legendary lead dog Togo, fifty miles out to meet the relay, but they weren't there. So out they went covering another fifty, and another, then another, and yet another. Finally he found the serum. The relay was abandoned because the weather had become impossible. So difficult was the relay in the harsh weather that one musher, Charlie Evans, harnessed himself to his sled after two of his dogs froze on their feet while mushing; should he too freeze, at least his body would be returned and not be lost on the trail - because the lead dogs always bring the team home. The deep snow, sub-zero temperatures, and white out conditions caused the trail to disappear. Alaskan storms are deadly.

In deep snow the dogs can only pull at a walking pace, struggling. The trail was gone; unable to see in the whiteout Seppala secured the serum on his sled and left the return to Togo. A good lead dog can find its own trail and sense danger.

Togo led the team out across the ice of Norton Sound, an unusually dangerous course due to the constantly shifting sea ice. If the wind shifted while Sep and his team were on the ice they could be lost at sea with no hope of being found. But the weather held and the trail across the ice stayed firm allowing Sep, Togo and the team to cut over a hundred miles and a full day of travel from the return. Nome was saved. Three hours after Togo led his team across the ice the wind shifted and the ice broke in Norton Sound.

Togo is the very great-great grandfather of my lead dogs Tasha and Ici. The stars shined on the lives of my sled dogs Blanca, Leto, and Ici. They each were born in the middle of the dates on which the great serum drive took place.

During that drive Togo worked harder than ever and covered over three-hundred forty miles. The miles took their toll on Togo making the nine-year old dog permanently lame and it was the last long run the little lead dog would make[2]. A good lead dog always brings the team home. The spirit of the Chukchi dog is strong - and God blesses their efforts.

Many know the near mythic story of Balto; mythic because Balto was a lead dog on Leonhard Seppala's second string team and was credited in stories for Togo's courage. Mushed by Gunnar Kaasen during the serum run, Balto's team was stationed at the final fifty mile mark to mush the final stretch into Nome; the point from which Seppala and Togo started their journey to find the serum. When Seppala and Togo returned from their legendary mush, they met Charlie Evans, who ran his dogs twenty five miles to meet Gunnar Kaasen and Balto handing the serum off to them. Balto led the last fifty miles into Nome. At Nome, Balto's team was met by journalists who wrote about the serum drive and credited Balto with the feat, because after all, it was Balto that brought the final team with the serum home to Nome.

Senator Dill of Washington made the serum drive part of the permanent Congressional record. One sentence of his record says "Men thought that the limit of speed and endurance had been reached in the grueling races of Alaska, but a race for sport and money proved far less stimulus than this contest, in which humanity was the urge and life was the prize."

Of Innisfree's Jim Brandenburg

I often called Brandenburg "Buddy' and he was the only male in the pack. He was a big husky with beautiful thick white fur with strawberry orange tips on his guard hairs. Aloof and proud, he loved to stay close to me, disinterested in other people. He would spend his days staring love-struck at Tasha, smiling with his eyes half closed. He would often laugh and prance around in a rocking-horse gait while Tasha was bossing the other huskies around, then she would come up to him wagging her tail, touching noses as if to say "See, aren't I the prettiest and best sled dog you've ever seen?"

Brandenburg was so content that he would always just sit or stand around smiling with his eyes half closed. A husky having eyes half closed is a submissive and carefree posture, one that he surely had because he believed that everything would always be okay. Brandenburg always had my love. Brandenburg had everything he could ever want. His days were filled with the company of the Currumpaws; the countless times running with the sled; and enjoying the beautiful sights of nature as he looked across his land. He would spend his time watching the amusing splendor of the antics of the four females, and smiling with eyes half closed because he was deeply in love with the strongest, smartest, and most beautiful girl on this earth, and Tasha loved him back. I could look at Brandenburg and his great joy would pass from him to me; for Brandenburg, life was perfect.

When Brandenburg was young, I mushed him in a two dog team with Tasha. We would run a six mile trail along a river, far from any sight of civilization. I trained him individually as a lead dog, and he quickly learned those skills, eventually passing them on to both Tasha and Ici. Unlike other working dogs, lead dogs best learn their skills from other lead dogs; how to turn left and right on the command of "haw" and "gee", how to find the trail and direction by scent; finding the fastest and hardest snow to make the work easier and save energy; keeping the team safe. A good lead dog always brings the team home.

Brandenburg did not run for much of the later part his life. One night while mushing all the huskies, we went out and covered only a half of a mile, and suddenly, Brandenburg stopped running. I knew from my experience with sled dogs that it meant that he needed to stop. Something was wrong with him; something was hurting him and he knew it was best not be maintain the fast pace that this fastest of teams could keep. I put him in the dog bag, which was always carried on the sled in case a dog injured itself on the trail, and we went back.

Huskies are most enthusiastic about the run in its earliest minutes. This is the time when they are most difficult to control and when commands to the lead dogs take a few seconds for them to process because they are so distracted with joy. I commanded Tasha to turn the team around at this early point in the run, with Brandenburg in the dog bag. Tasha pulled the team around from the right to return to where we started, obeying my command, "Tasha, gee round!" A good lead dog always brings the team home - even when they don't want to.

Later I found out that Brandenburg had epilepsy and the mental stress of running with the team was not comfortable for him. That's why he stopped running that night.

Once Tasha and Ici were hitched as a lead team, their learning continued as a result of friendly competition. Ici knew that Tasha was my favorite, and she knew that Tasha would obey any command and do anything to please me. When they ran together it was apparent that there was always a competition between them to see who could obey my commands the fastest, with the most physically expressed demonstration of completing the command followed by a prideful and taunting look to the other leader.

A Day in the Life of a Currumpaw

The huskies antics and expressions were priceless. Huskies laugh, and they express extreme joy by running in a rocking horse gait. At play, their facial expressions include taunting, defiance, and outright silliness. The would play and talk at each other in these taunting, rolling tones and make silly faces at each other—their absolute love for each other was so apparent, they each felt it and they loved what they were.

Standing with the huskies on their land, I'd be overwhelmed with a sense of togetherness as each of the huskies would look me right in the eye with an expression of pleasure, love, and adoration. I couldn't help but feel that to them I was the most wonderful sight and the most beautiful thing. They each looked at me with an expression that was fitting of each of their individual personalities; sweet Brandenburg staring in my direction with his eyes half closed – smiling; Blanca wagging her tail wildly and looking as if to say "aren't I cute - come pet me!"; Leto with the look a warrior showing me not just a look of love but one of pride and respect; and Ici with a stoic expression with total concentration - the aloofness of a true sled dog. And then there was Tasha, who would look into my eyes with an expression of absolute adoration, so moving because she was stunningly beautiful—so perfect she was that she looked like a stuffed animal, her perfect little feet totally covered in thick fur that showed no trace of claws or toes, just like stuffed animal feet.

The huskies were bred as show dogs and this was evident in their gate. Each of the huskies moved so perfectly, with head held high, ears pointed up, and with a prideful gate not usually seen in other breeds. They moved in this posture and seemed to float rather than walk. I loved to watch them float like this; it was not just stunning but it made me proud and I would just smile. This perfection in their gate not only meant that they moved perfectly, but they moved efficiently and effortlessly which translated into speed and endurance on the trail.

Their favorite game was wolf tag, which included an endless variety of athletic moves to dodge the pursuer, garnished with the funny faces they would make at each other. I would sit and watch them play for hours, often laughing hysterically as one husky would sneak up on another, with its head and body low, "tip-toeing" up behind another and scare it with a great pouncing leap. Embarrassed, the other husky would turn - and the pursuit was on again, often with each of them laughing and running in that silly rocking horse gait.

The huskies didn't need the other huskies to play because they knew how to play by themselves. A favorite game to play alone was for a husky to grab a toy, which could be anything from a rawhide bone, a rock, or even a piece of bark found outside. The husky would stalk it, sneak up on it, and finally begin pouncing around it in circles woofing at it and finally attacking it. Then the husky might grab it and run off with it, later throwing it up in the air and catching it. Sometimes the husky would throw it and miss the catch, pretending to be surprised by its escape and the stalking would start all over again.

The huskies received plenty of affection – from each of the other huskies and from me. It was the most loving experience to live with the Currumpaws, so much so that while petting each of them, a song came from my heart to celebrate each of their lives. I would sing little songs to them and each husky had a their own song. They loved the way the language brought my thoughts to focus on their spirit and persona. They loved that the songs repeated their names over and over. It may be hard for people to understand but in song, like singing in church, your soul opens and your true feelings and heart come out. The huskies loved me more for it.

For Brandenburg, Mr. Brandenburg, his song was beautiful and sad—but he absolutely loved to hear it. It was to the melody of Edelweiss. He longed for the mush, but his body told him that it was too much stress for him, and the song reflected that which was missing in his life.

For Tasha, the song was silly. "Tasha KO, Tasha Ko, pulls a sled, any size, Tasha Ko!" For Blanca, it was equally silly. Sung to the melody of Casper the Friendly Ghost, "Blanca the friendly dog, the friendliest dog we know, Blanca paw, Blanca paw, Blanca, Blanca, Blanca paw."

For Leto, it was the rough song I once heard in a Star Trek movie, a Klingon melody. In Star Trek, the Klingons were a great warrior race; Leto was a great warrior. It was a rough and masculine song and she loved it. For Ici, her song was just silly, stating her name over and over. Ici the Ice Dancer, Ici the Ice Dancer, Ici the Ice Dancer, Ici—Ici—Ici.

I would pet each of the huskies often every day, but I also used to hug them, coming up from behind and wrapping my arms around the thick ruff of their neck and chest, lifting and squeezing them so that their forepaws lifted off the ground. This pleased them, and it also reinforced my place as the master of the pack.

Most mushers raise their dogs by keeping them in a dog yard, and area where each dog is "staked out" - attached to a stake in the ground with a type of dog-house that they could also for privacy and warmth. The Currumpaws were raised as a pack and as sled dogs, but they were also pets. They slept in the house with me and liked their time in the house, enjoying their togetherness and being near their master.

While the Currumpaws developed a large vocabulary and responded to many different types of commands including hand signals, one of the most fascinating things about them was the way they responded appropriately when no commands of any kind were given. They liked to go in and out of the house to play outside or do their doggy duties. I could walk to the door without a command and any husky that wanted to go outside would just follow. They spent their time in a kennel room when I was away. When it was time for me to leave the house I would just walk toward the kennel room and they would all follow, each going into their individual kennels - standing there smiling at me.

My huskies were trained to have house manners and the behavior that was accepted in the house was different than what was allowable outside on their land. They could play and do anything they wanted outside, but inside they were required to be on good behavior, which they willingly did because they loved the togetherness. Huskies were naturally energy conserving dogs and they would spend their time in the house relaxing and sleeping. The Chukchis kept their best huskies in their yarangas, a round tent, and also in their more permanent homes where they had small herds of reindeer. Amongst their primitive instincts of the pack and the predator, was an instinct to be compatible with the every day life of humans. This made them perfectly suited to life in the house. As I walked around the house, I walked with a group of huskies around my feet following me everywhere - how comical that must have looked to visitors. They did; however, have other favorite pastimes in the house.

I have a big kitchen, and they love watching dinner be cooked. They would huddle around my feet and move with me, never getting in the way. They never begged food from the table because food never went from the table to a husky. Had I allowed that, the big pack might surely take over. They sat at attention while I was cooking because they would get scraps. It was one of the highlights of their day. Leto especially liked to get the leaves of lettuce I would toss her while making salads. Each husky would catch the lettuce while it was in air, and Leto would catch hers and shake it violently over and over, "killing" it before she ate it.

Any Evening—Any Night

The night is late and its time for bed. The five Currumpaw Siberians file into my bedroom, each with its own special place; Tasha sleeping on the floor next to me, Brandenburg by the door, Blanca in the corner and Leto on the far left corner of the bed. Ici would sit on the opposite of Leto, which would be on my right. Ici would sit there with her chin up and the most annoyed look on her face, waiting for me to get into bed. Chin up because when I finally slipped into the covers she would raise her chin and stretch her neck over my right leg laying her head down with a great big sigh and resting her head there the rest of the night.

Silence? No. Every night I would hear a concert, the rhythmic sound of the five huskies breathing. So comforting I would fall asleep; by sleeping together, the pack bonds. The Chukchi people believed that a man's wealth was demonstrated by the quality and love of his sled dogs and the team. I would sometimes remember this as I would fall asleep to that rhythmic sound and think to myself, "Who could be richer than I?"

Any Morning—Any Day

Each morning the huskies would wake, and Tasha would celebrate the day as she did every day - letting out a big moan for her huskies to know it was time to get up. She would jump in the air with a half twist and a big smile, then she would roll on her back, wiggling and scratching her back. Then she would lay there on her back and watch me - upside down.

I would have breakfast and, when finished, just sit and relax. Without a word or an action from me, a hysteria would break out; the huskies knew I was thinking about taking them mushing. How would they know? They always knew what I was thinking; it's a mystery to this day. This is how it always was, any time, day or night.

The huskies loved living in the house just as much as they loved spending time outside. They loved watching the day to day activities and enjoyed us all being together. They would run outside with great enthusiasm and return with equally enthused. They were perfectly suited for the cold or rain, but they loved the house too.

One day the temperature dropped to forty below zero, a rarity in this temperate land. Brandenburg wanted to go outside in the dog yard so I let him out. He walked out through the snow into the bitter cold, with the wind blowing strong and setting a chill factor far below one hundred degrees below zero. After a short while I called for him to come back but he was standing far to the back of the land gazing over his territory. I checked on him several times, but each time he wanted to stay out. With these cold temperatures, I began to become concerned about him; I called for him once again, and he just looked over at me and didn't budge. I decided to go out and get him.

I walked to the back of the huskies' land where he was standing and there he stood with the wind in his face and a great big smile and his eyes half closed. He didn't want to come in because these bitter temperatures were unusual for us and standing out there must have sparked something in his instincts. He just stood there smiling. What was he thinking? I imagined he was just enjoying the bitter cold, the howling wind and blowing snow, and thinking to himself, "This is perfect; this is home."

I touched him gently on the back of the neck which is a dominant gesture the huskies were accustomed to meaning they should follow me and he immediately went with me into the house. Once inside, he walked up to a window and stared outside for a very long time.

I spent so much time with the huskies that I was in touch with their thoughts and feelings. But this demonstration of Brandenburg's attraction to the bitter cold was one that I will never truly know; I can only guess. The Chukchis called the little dogs "Spirit Dogs." Perhaps Brandenburg knew that this harsh weather which is so threatening to human life were the conditions in which the little Chukchi sled dogs shined. Weather such as this had created the times throughout history when the little dogs were the last hope for the People. In these times the sled dogs stepped up and made their great contributions to the survival of the Tribe.

The Complete Sled Dog

The social order of the pack is strong with each member having a special and important place. As civilized humans it is difficult for us to relate to the culture of predatory animals. Predators have their own special needs, which are unlike our needs, and they fight. Today, even with knowledge of field biologists and other scientists, we still try to anthropomorphize animals and do what we want with wild animals, regardless of their nature. Civilized man, for the most part, is more ignorant of nature and wildlife today than at any other time in history.

Recently, people began taking on wolves as pets and breeding hybrid wolves, which are part dog and part wolf. Breeders have promoted their breeding as being a certain percentage wolf as if it were some attractive quality. The wolf is wild and has no place with humans. Certainly we can share the land with the wolf, but it is not in our or the wolf's nature to cohabitate with each other. People buy these creatures as pets, which usually leads to the creature's demise when the owners start experiencing all the uncivilized parts of the wolf.

Wolves need a great deal of land to sustain themselves and they are not comfortable living as we do. Keeping a wolf on a plot of land, perhaps a nice forty acre spread, would be akin to us raising our children in a closet. An inevitable neurosis develops which is soon followed by the demise of the animal. This attempt at domestication creates an emptiness in the lives of captive wolves – the unfulfilled desire to live as a wolf.

Wolfers and the native people have nothing good to say about this practice. Native people are close to the land and nature, which comprises the strongest part of their overall spiritual beliefs. Wolfers are those who hunt wolves for bounty; wolves are elusive creatures and to be successful hunters wolfers must understand the wolf. I do not approve of wolfing, but it has always been government sanctioned and we must recognize people for the skills they have and the knowledge they have attained. The native people cannot comprehend why anyone would want to confine what is free, preventing it from doing what God intended it to do; live with the pack, hunt, sustain the pack through time, and be one with Nature.

Regarding the percentage of wolf that a hybrid is, the wolfers say, if it acts like a wolf - it's a wolf. The difference between wolves and dogs, including sled dogs, is that wolves prefer the company of wolves.

The sled dogs, these beautiful, loving animals, have all the attributes of the other domesticated dogs and of course prefer the company of people. They are, however, predators and have been bred pure for three thousand years and with that comes attributes that are not familiar to us - the total concentration and single- mindedness of the predator.

The Currumpaw huskies loved each other, a very strong love between each member of the pack—and they loved the pack. They loved being together, they loved mushing and every little experience we had. But huskies fight. When huskies fight, they make the most horrible and vicious sound, and the fights are aggressive. They would fight over anything - even who would get to sniff a blade of grass first.

The fights are how the pack maintains its order. Leto, the Beta, was the strongest and most aggressive, but Tasha, the Alpha, was highly intelligent and had an athletic prowess that was stunning. Fights between the Alpha and Beta were rare and Tasha was very non-confrontational with regard to Leto. Sometimes Leto would be in the mood to start a fight with her and Tasha would sense it. Tasha would walk by Leto turning her head away so as not to make eye contact with her. In this way she paid respect to Leto's position and prowess. She was not submitting to Leto, but these gestures gave Leto even greater confidence as the Alpha.

Ici and Leto were always together and always getting into something. They had the type of friendship we all long for, every minute of every day was fun for them and they loved being together - they were litter mates. But sled dogs must follow their instincts and the two would fight often. Ici was no match for the powerful Leto but she wouldn't stand down during a fight, which she almost always began losing within the first few seconds. Sometimes Leto would have no choice but to grab her by the neck and pin her down onto the ground and not let her up until she totally submitted. Leto, though, never hurt Ici.

One beautiful Thanksgiving day after a substantial snowfall I let Leto and Ici play outside in the snow. It was common for the two of them to spend a great deal of time outside especially when there was nice snow to run and play in. Leto and Ici got into a fight and of course Leto was the victor, but the fight happened outside without my knowledge. There were no injuries except for a few small teeth marks. Ice had a puncture on the top of her head and I could tell that it hurt a little. As it healed, it created scar tissue under her scalp, and her head swelled up like a big balloon. It almost looked funny, but Ici was obviously uncomfortable. The pack's veterinarian, Dr. Wolf, treated her and everything turned out just fine. But huskies remember. From that day on Ici held a grudge against Leto and the two had to be separated and could not be left alone unattended. It broke my heart to see them always apart because they had been such good friends and pack mates. At least they were okay to be together in the house, because the house rules were that there was minimum play and certainly no fighting. Even after this Ici and Leto would often huddle together napping.

Blanca was the Omega. She was a big dog and fought dirty. All the Currumpaw sled dogs were actually afraid of her. She was the Omega because she chose to be; she was simply not smart enough to have a higher place in the pack. Being the Omega, she would submit to each of the other huskies, putting her tail between her legs, head down lower than the other dog's, and lick at their lips while whining, confirming their higher places in the pack.

When sled dogs fight, like wolves, rarely is there any type of injury. Blanca did not fight to change her position in the pack, she fought simply because she could—and liked to. If two huskies got into a fight, sometimes she would run towards the fight as fast as she could and join in. This annoyed me as well as the fighting huskies, and breaking up a three way fight was much more difficult. I could pull one off, then trying to break up the other two only to have the first dog jump back in on the remaining one, a vicious and endless circle.

Brandenburg did not like to fight, even though he was by far the biggest. One day Leto jumped him and there Brandenburg was, with this look of absolute horror and terror on his face, standing on his hind legs backed up against a fence, unable to believe that she jumped him. He wouldn't fight back. There was something different about Brandenburg; he was sweet and loving beyond imagination. I scolded Leto, and she sat with this sorrowful look on her face realizing what she had done.

The one thing mushers hate the most were "dog box fights". Sled dogs travel to races in trucks that have dog boxes integrated into their sides with access doors from the outside of the truck. Often mushers would put two dogs in each box. Suddenly you could hear that terrible sound, a dog fight - in the box. You would have no choice but to stick your arm in there blindly and grab one of them and pull them out, surely being bitten accidentally each time.

The huskies don't mean to bite you but the fights are so fast and furious that the dogs bite at anything. The few times I was bitten the dog that bit me by accident knew it and would sit and look at me so sorrowfully, feeling really bad. The bites don't hurt much and are never so bad as to cause injuries—this level of control is instinctual to them. Fighting is not the hunt, fighting is the way of the pack.

I never lost my temper with the dogs because they never really did anything wrong - fighting is part of what makes sled dogs what they are. Fighting is part of what gives them the fortitude to endure the extreme difficulties of the trail and is the true test of maintaining an appropriate position in the pack. The order of the pack is strong and it is a living order constantly validating itself.

On the Trail

Huskies love to run at night when they are guided by their greater sense of smell and comforted by the lower temperatures. When we took longer runs, perhaps over thirty miles, they were always night journeys. At night everything is quiet and the trail is well illuminated from the ambient light reflected off the snow. When the moon was high the trail was as bright as day, casting crisp shadows of the team on the trail.

One of the most memorable things about mushing was bringing the dogs to their position on the sled's gang line one by one. In the early days, I would first bring Tasha out, who would keep tension on the gang line, the line that strung them out and attached them all together, while the other dogs were brought out. Upon bringing the second dog, they would start singing in excited yelps, howls, and barks, impatient for the mush. Blanca would never shut her mouth, saying yaaa eeeh hooo waah rouw rouw endlessly; very comical actually. As if the screaming weren't enough, Leto and Blanca would leap forward as hard as they could, thinking that it would get the sled going, but the sled is anchored in the ice, or attached with a "snub line" to an immovable object. Instead of moving forward their jumping just had the affect of sending them slightly airborne, landing each of them right back where they started. Tasha would always have the most annoyed look on her face because the extra tension on the gangline went right to her collar, and she too was trying to concentrate on singing and whining.

Each of the dog's songs grew louder as each dog was brought out and hitched to the gangline. Finally, Brandenburg would be brought out and the songs would keep growing louder still because now they knew the mush was only seconds away. A husky's patience is completely thrown aside when faced with the prospect of doing the thing they loved most. Upon giving Tasha the forward command, "let's go", this loud yelping and howling would suddenly turn to absolute silence, and all I could hear was the sound of the accelerating runners sliding on the snow and all I could feel was the unrestrained energy of the pack. Speed and silence. Mushers have a favorite saying, "Run silent, run dogs."

Every time we finished a run, I would rub each of the huskies' ruff, the thick fur around their neck, and pet their heads telling each of them what good sled dogs they were. Praise they didn't even need because they had been doing what they loved to do most, what they were born to do, and they loved me for being there with them. But the pack culture was one where greetings were always joyous and I treated the finish of a run with the same joyous greetings we would have when we were apart - they loved the praise and it reinforced the togetherness of the pack and their sense of purpose.

There were many days and nights of mushing with the Currumpaws, and I was always careful not to run them too often. They always had a full day of rest between long mushes. In this way their bodies could get stronger, building just the way athletes do. After these long mushes they would get lots of extra food to support the strengthening of their muscles. They never ran tired and this was one of the secrets to their success in races.

Our favorite place to run was a five mile long trail near the huskies' land. The trail was high over a valley and you could see for miles, even the tall buildings of the city twenty miles to the north. The view was stunning at night, especially when the moon was out. The sea of stars that the Chukchi called the "Pebbly River", what we call the Milky Way, was bright above. The Currumpaws were fast. One night, after the snow had been settled for a few days and the sun made the trail hard and icy we ran with a speed I never experienced again. The huskies and I ran the ten miles out and back, even while stopping to cross some roads, in less than thirty minutes. When I finally stopped the sled I let Tasha string the huskies' gang line tight and I pet and praised each of them as I always did. It was always thrilling to run the dogs. It was a true blessing to have these experiences with my pack.

The five mile long trail actually went much further, crossing a busy state road and going on for many more miles. There were many instances that my lead dog Tasha performed perfectly saving the team and me from harm. We experienced this on this very trail one night.

One beautiful winter night we headed out on the trail. The snow was perfect and the trail was well packed from cross country skiers and snowmobiles. The moon was bright and it seemed as if daylight illuminated the open valley. The huskies were running perfectly and I enjoyed the scenery in the bright conditions. Eventually we came to the five mile point where we normally turn around and I decided to go further and enjoy the moment. The trail crosses a busy road and then continues right through a new housing development before re-entering the woods. This was an enjoyable section simply because of the novelty of running through this neighborhood.

Just before reaching the busy road the trail runs through a parking lot for people who come to use the trail. To cross a road I would approach the road slowly and use the sled brake to bring the team to a complete halt. Crossing roads at night was much easier than daytime crossing because of the reduced traffic and the headlights of approaching cars could be seen at a great distance. We reached the parking lot and I hit the sled brake to slow the team. Suddenly I was struck with fear as I realized the brake would have no effect on the sled because the many cars using the parking lot had in the day had turned the snow into sheer, hard ice.

I pushed the brake as hard as I could but it had no effect on the speeding team. I began giving Tasha the "whoa" command to make her stop, but this is the one command lead dogs have difficulty with, if they can even obey at all, because they don't understand why you would want to stop. Under normal conditions the sled brake stops the team. The sled brake also creates a dominant gesture, one of great force which the team seems to enjoy as it assures them that their master is in control. I kept yelling the "whoa" command, but the lead dogs did not respond. There are other things a musher can do, such as lay the sled over, but that would have had little affect on the hard ice.

We were very rapidly approaching the road and I was struck with terror, afraid for my huskies which I loved with all my heart. The road was wide with cars traveling well over fifty miles per hour. It were as if my life were passing before me and I imagined the team being struck by a speeding car leaving a bloody horrible mess with huskies torn apart and writhing in pain. Huskies looking to me to make everything all right and me running in circles struck with horror and grief, scurrying mindlessly in the traffic trying to triage my little dogs - unable to make everything all right.

These thought and emotions ran strong and I screamed at Tasha to stop, suddenly she realized by my voice and the senses that huskies have that this command was urgent and I was truly stricken with fright which was heightened by my love for the team. Tasha dug those stuffed animal feet into the ice with her neck line yanking Ici to make her stop, the wheel dogs running right into the lead pair immediately followed by the sled. I grabbed the neckline that attaches the two lead dogs and now the team was safe. I looked at Tasha and there she stood with the most serious look on her face trying to understand my fear. I hugged her and told her what a great lead dog she was and I praised all the huskies. A good lead dog makes sure the team can come home.

One very cold winter, I decided to take the team out over the ice. This became the ultimate test of Tasha's ability as a lead dog. Lakes are deadly and occasionally we would hear of a musher breaking through the ice and him and his team losing their life and the lives of their team. The ice was thick so I saw no harm in taking the team out over the open ice field. It was fun and plenty fast. Not having a trail to follow, it was especially fun giving the lead dogs commands on the open ice, and watching them follow the command. It was really good training for them. Suddenly I realized that the snow on top of the ice was getting to be a darker color. This part of the lake must have been affected by a warm current. I did not panic and I slowed the team, but did not stop them as this would have placed greater pressure on the weakened ice. Tasha could feel the wet snow and began turning the team in a large arc, her eyes occasionally looking down at the ice, her head tilting back and forth to hear the sound of the ice. Finally she was able to move the team around the dangerous ice, finding the hard ice and we sped back to shore. She really was a great lead dog, a thinking dog. Tasha always brought the team home. I never dared the ice again.

Brandenburg was the first lead dog and he had a good sense of the trail. He never ran on soft ice or other areas where the team might get their feet wet. In these days Tasha ran lead next to her love; days I'm sure that were the most close to her heart. In those days Ici was still learning the ways of the mush and I had her placed next to Leto in the "wheel" position closest to the sled, with Blanca running the "swing" position alone between the lead and wheel pairs.

One day while mushing the very young Currumpaws in a state forest, a swivel failed on the gang line that connected all the dogs, breaking right between Leto in the swing position, and the two wheel dogs, Blanca and Ici. The sled slowed and off went the two leaders with Leto. They were excited and would not heed my commands to return. The temperature was dropping quickly below zero, and I began to suffer from the cold. Ici and Blanca were not strong enough to keep up with the three loose dogs, so we returned to camp.

I radioed for help from the park rangers who patrolled the land on snowmobiles. I was frightened for my three missing huskies and I was growing weak from the cold. Hypothermia was beginning to set in.

I returned to the place where we began the run and after a while I heard the sound of something coming; there was a park ranger who had attached the dogs to the front of his snowmobile letting them lead the snowmobile back to where I was. The ranger detached the dogs, and while walking toward me I noticed the great pride that came from him. It was not only the pride that came from the ranger successfully performing his duty, it was pride that came from him because he was so moved by the experience of being led by the small team, and to be walking in the presence of these great dogs, and I felt his happiness as he returned the huskies to me.

In days past, certainly well before the days of this ranger, park rangers had used dog teams to move around the parks. As time passed, the park service replaced the sled dog with the snowmobile. The park ranger knew this, and he went home with the happy experience of finding the sled dogs and living some of what the park rangers before his time had experienced.

The park ranger was so happy with the experience that when the park shot a promotional film they called me and the Currumpaw Siberians to the park to be filmed. Through this film many people were able to see the splendor of the Currumpaws.

Tasha was the best lead dog, and could sense danger on the trail. One day while mushing through a national park, we came to the top of a hill and Tasha stopped the team. She refused to go further and ignored my repeated commands. Knowing the sled dog as I do, I gave her the command that turns the team around from her right – "Tasha, gee-round!" She turned the team and we started back on the winding trail. Suddenly I heard a sound I don't normally hear, one that is unmistakable to me - the hypersonic sound of rifle fire. There were poachers nested in the trees waiting for deer; poachers because hunting was prohibited in the park except by rangers and contracted hunters who used crossbows to prevent stray shots from hurting park visitors. The sight of a dog team emerging from the trees is surely one that a poacher did not expect. Were they wolves, or perhaps coyotes? Surely the sight of a sled dog team would have taken them by surprise and they could have easily made a mistake and fired upon us. I believe that Tasha was a lead dog as great as any that had ever lived. She was a good lead dog and she always brought the team home.

Racing didn't produce the stories and memories that everyday running did, except for the fact that races were run at high speed. Races are run with smaller teams running first, single dogs for new mushers and children, three dog, four dog, then finally the six dog class.

Before the Currumpaw Siberians raced in their first race, the other mushers knew they were going to be fast because there were some days that we trained together and my huskies' speed was apparent. The mushers were most concerned about the competition in the "four dog" races. When the team entered one of the largest races in the region, the mushers saw that they were registered for the "four dog" class. What they didn't notice was that the Currumpaws were entered in the "three dog" class as well and there were only four of them that I raced. Brandenburg just came along for the ride. To everyone's surprise, the three dogs that ran the three dog class were entered in the four dog class with Tasha added to complete the team. The light grey Tasha was not as fast as the three light red huskies, Ici, Leto, and Blanca. Leto ran the wheel position closest to the sled, with Ici leading. With Tasha being fresh in the four dog class, she would motivate them to run faster than they might have without her.

In their first major race, the weather was very cold and it had been snowing for days. The sub zero temperatures made the deep snow very soft and created difficult trail conditions. But the Currumpaws were fit to run much longer distances and they dominated the three dog class winning by over eight minutes. To everyone's surprise, the Currumpaws entered the four dog class immediately afterwards and placed second. I couldn't have been more proud of the little dogs. They were bred to be show dogs rather than racing dogs but had proved that good training, enthusiasm, and their strong pack instincts were the keys to their success.

The three dog class was always run before the four dog class, a tradition that would dictate the successes of the Currumpaws for the rest of their time in races. We experienced great success in the three dog class and near wins in the four dog class. I never ran the four dog class fresh because I didn't care about winning, and my huskies loved to run the fresh course a few times; a course that was new to them and to a sled dog—a new adventure from our everyday trails.

There were always spectators at the races; families bringing their children to see and enjoy the huskies and experience the excitement of the race and the mush. Of all the spectators, I don't think anyone enjoyed the races as much as did the Amish.

There was once a race across Amish country organized by a slightly elderly woman who also raced and lived with Siberians. She called me and asked me to help her gain permission from the Amish to traverse their land. Gaining approval from the Amish was the easiest task you could imagine. After all, a race powered by dogs which demonstrates the bond between the animal and the musher was an "English[3]" sport they could relate to.

She asked me to help her gain permission because that is a task that is difficult for a woman to do. The Amish would readily grant her permission, but an Amish man who was head of a household was almost always married and it is inappropriate for him to speak directly to an English woman. She would have to stand at the door and messages would be relayed back and forth by the Amish wife or one of her daughters. The Amish don't mind doing this, but it is a slight inconvenience to distract two family members from their work. I was accustomed to dealing with the Amish and their suspicions of the English so I was happy to visit the families and enjoy the pleasant conversations with them.

Rather than drive to their homes in my truck, I would walk across their land to each home, which made them immediately more comfortable with me. Once an Amish man proudly invited me to walk across his farm to see how well he was preparing the farm for next year's planting and harvest. His teenage son was plowing the fields with a single draft horse. Even though I was accustomed to the Amish, I had never had the opportunity to observe the plow horse in action.

The boy would turn one short row at a time, allowing the horse to rest before turning the next row. It was wonderful seeing the boy and his horse working together. We had a great time talking about the care and use of the plow horse and I shared with him the care and use of the sled dog.

When the day of the race came the entire Amish community gathered at the back side of the race course drinking cider and snacking on cheese; cheering and clapping as each musher and team passed. It was a great day for them, their community and their families enjoying this spectacle brought to their land. Perhaps those English weren't so bad after all.

I never knew if the Currumpaws realized that they won races. They only knew that each run was wonderful and they put all their hearts and souls into each run, loving the running, the wilderness, and endless smells that would pass them, being together, and serving me. After each race I praised them as I always did; for them each run was perfect - as each run really was for me as well, and I thought that the huskies were perfect too.

The Cycle of Life

Something happened to Leto, she started to lose weight. I began giving her shots of insulin and she had to go out every two hours. At night she would wake me silently by moving over to me and quietly sitting next to me while I slept, which would be just enough to wake me and I would take her out - every two hours, every night. This went on for a year. She loved me, but in these days, as if it were even possible, she loved me more - loyalty repaid. She showed it to me with her eyes. I would go to the door to let her out and she would look up at me with the most beautiful adoration. I could have separated Leto by placing her and one of the other huskies in the kennel room but I preferred to wake up and take care of my pack rather than isolating Leto and denying her the pleasure of the bonding that occurs when the pack sleeps together. I wanted her to spend her nights in togetherness with all the huskies and be comforted by the rhythmic concert of their breathing.

As time went on, Leto's body continued to fail. The ears with which she could hear danger were no longer as sharp. The eyes with which she saw and embraced the wonders of the world grew cloudy. The muscles that once provided her great strength grew smaller and weaker, but still carried her with a pride such as I have never seen. But her heart grew stronger and her face was more beautiful than ever. I would watch her go outside by herself, and I would say to myself in absolute heartbreak, "Oh my poor Leto."

As through her entire life, she fought until the end. She died young, why her? Why the strongest? Why the one who loved life more than any other? When she would look up at me with those adoring eyes, she really believed that I could make everything all right and part of me believes that because she believed it, I somehow failed her, I could never make things all right for her.

It was difficult for me to bear the sorrow of Leto's passing, but I believe with all my heart that I was not alone with the knowledge of the passing of this great animal's life. At the very moment of Leto's death I heard the most disturbing sound - a siren, then a loud screech and a boom. I walked to the front of my property and there I saw the dead body of a deer that had been struck by a speeding police car. Flying through the air from the impact, it landed on my lawn - Leto's home. The deer is the other part of the symbiotic relationship that Leto, a predator, had with nature. The Earth praised her, mourning her passing in this way, and praised me for my loyalty to her during her time of sickness. The deer totem, the deer spirit, gave up a life in recognition and remembrance of Leto.

I buried Leto on her land, and wrote on her collar of her brave experiences not all told in this story, "protector of life, lust for life as no other". I buried her in a special place where she liked to gaze over her land and see the rolling orchards and the woods. I buried her where she could see the beautiful sunset as the sun lowered over the orchards and where the deer, the fox, and all the wild animals pass by. The four huskies watched me as I gently lowered her into her grave - and they knew where she was.

The order of the pack is strong with each member having a special and important place. Leto was the protector of the pack. While at home she would sleep in her private place under a small table. She would wake at short intervals and tour the house; checking the doors, windows, and anywhere a scent might indicate an intruder - an invader of her territory. She would look to see where each member of her pack was and when satisfied she would return to her private place and relax. Even though she was buried in this beautiful place on her land with the occasional company of the passing wildlife, it broke my heart to think of her sleeping there without her pack - alone.

A Husky Howls

Wolves and huskies howl for many reasons, some of which are surely unknown to us. But we do know that they howl to try to determine where members of the pack are and that they howl in unison, each in a different pitch creating a wonderful lupine musical chord making the pack seem larger than it is.

Blanca had lost her daughter and friend, and after Leto was buried she didn't like to come into the house. She would sit outside near where Leto was buried, her little girl. Huskies howl, but Blanca would sit by Leto's grave and let out these awful, long, mournful howls; remembering, missing her little girl, and perhaps hoping that her Leto would return to her. If that was so, she never lost that hope. Perhaps one day she will once again be reunited with Leto.

Brandenburg was the oldest and passed a few months later. His was a happy and joyful life. He was the sweetest dog to walk this earth. The three huskies watched me as I buried my buddy on his land next to Leto. I placed my hand on the heavy cut stone that marked where Leto has been sleeping without her pack and looked through the earth toward her and gave her just a little sad smile. From this day on Leto does not sleep alone.

Of Currumpaw's Natasha Ko

Tasha was my favorite, all her life she barely did anything wrong. Like her legendary grandfather, Innisfree's Pegasus, she was never any trouble. Tasha was always at my side. Sometimes she would like to take this further and overly submit to me, in as much a dominating posture as a submissive one. While I would be sitting she would often climb right up onto me, forepaws first, and lick my face over and over. She especially liked to sneak up on me if I were lying on the floor watching the television. She would pounce on me holding my neck down with one forepaw and my forehead down with the other then start licking my face.

Siberian Huskies are beautiful, but Tasha was uncommonly beautiful. Tasha stood strong and proud, her strength and beauty shining through - she was the Alpha female.

Tasha liked to play fetch with her little yellow football. She would chase and return it a million times. If I threw it at her to catch I would put my hand out and she would throw it back to me - right into my hand. If I didn't play fetch with her, she would bring me the football and force it into my hand.

Tasha was my best lead dog and I suspect she was one of the best lead dogs that ever lived. One time we were crossing a lake with Tasha leading when the ice began to break; Tasha quickly steered the team across ice that was safe. There were many other times we fell into danger on the trail; a good lead dog she could always sense danger, and find a safe trail. Tasha always brought the team home.

The native People say that there are many trails in life; the only good trail to follow is that of a good human being. My lead dog reminded me of this on every mush; it will be difficult to follow her trail, her great courage, her great joy for life, the great love she had for the pack, and the love she had for me.

Tasha, being the great lead dog that she was, had a sense for all things around her; she needed to be in control. One day Blanca jumped her, and Blanca being the dirty fighter that she was, tore Tasha's lower left eye lid. I took Tasha to Dr. Wolf and he stitched her up. Dr. Wolf was not the local veterinarian, he was the caretaker of the Currumpaw pack and I had to drive far to see him. He had to anesthetize Tasha to stitch her eye, and just let me take her home while she was unconscious.

She went to sleep in the operating room and woke in my living room with a look of total confusion. To a lead dog that is in touch with everything around her, this was too much to bear - "how could I be here, when I was just there?" I'm sure she thought. From that day on she did not like to go into any room in the vet's office.

All the mushers were jealous of Tasha and of the Currumpaw wins. I really didn't have the huskies to race, but to share my life with, experience the behavior of the pack first hand, and run them. Racing was just a way for them to see other dogs and be exposed to lots of spectators who would admire them. Because they are difficult to control, sled dogs were prohibited from walking off lead at dog sled races and weren't supposed to leave the staging area. But the race officials were proud of Tasha and at races I would rub salt in the mushers' wounds by taking Tasha with me everywhere - off lead.

At one race I walked into the cabin, and left her outside on a deck. When I returned, there she stood, with this funny look on her face, a loving and unbelievably content look. Six or seven small children surrounded her, each only two or three years old and barely taller than she. Each child had a hand on her; petting her, touching her, Tasha standing there smiling - I will always remember her this way.

When Tasha was barely an adolescent, a friend of mine left one of his belongings at my house so I took Tasha with me for a quick stop at a dance studio to return it. Tasha was instantly surrounded by ballet dancers doting over her. Tasha, looking up at them smiling was totally distracted and she didn't hear, or didn't listen to me say its time to go, so I left anyway. This would be a good lesson for her because as a lead dog her attention should be on me. While walking away I looked back down the hall to the door I had come out of and there Tasha came, a comical look on her face - shooting out the door sliding sideways on the slippery floor with her legs still scrambling in a direction different from her slide, and a look of worry and total focus as she scrambled to the place and feeling she loved most, to be at my side. For the rest of her life she never lost focus on me or where I was and would run to my side with just the wave of my finger, looking at me with an expression of happiness and pride and hoping that I would ask her to do something for me.

Tasha was the Alpha female and had a thirst for the hunt as no other in the pack. While mushing, deer would often pass and Tasha wanted dearly to be cut loose and go after the herd. A good lead dog, she fought her instincts and kept about her business of mushing, turning her head repeatedly to watch the deer. She wanted to run after the herd and I could feel the longing in her heart for the chase.

One night I went for a walk on the huskies' land with Tasha off lead. It was very dark and I didn't notice the eight or nine deer standing in the orchards. Tasha bolted toward the herd and disappeared into the woods, hot on the trail of the deer - her long sought after hunt was on! Of course being a small dog she didn't catch any deer. Being a good lead dog, and the Alpha of the pack, she found her way home after a very short time.

The next day I took Tasha for another walk off lead on the huskies land. I walked with her often but I this time noticed something very different about her. She was a very proud dog, and knew that she was the Alpha. Her strength and beauty was always stunning, but this day she walked at my side with a gait and a pride that I had never before seen from her. After all, on this day her dream had been realized; she had pursued the herd. Somehow, a little part of her hopes and dreams had been fulfilled and I was happy for her.

Tasha was uncommonly intelligent and this was evident in every day life. When a husky wants to come in from outside, it makes little yelps to let me know it waited at the door. When Tasha wanted to come in from outside she would knock at the door. When Blanca was a little puppy I would often keep her in a cage I used to help train her. The cage had two latches to keep the husky in. To open the latch you had to lift it up and slide it to the right. Blanca kept getting out of her cage and I could not understand how. To solve this mystery I spied on her and discovered that Tasha was the culprit! Tasha would walk up to the cage and, in an instant, flip up the latch and slide it over letting Blanca out. Tasha could open the cage faster than I could.

When Tasha grew old she became sick but, fortunately, I was blessed with several extra months with her. During her illness time she got lots of extra attention and we played many games of fetch with her little yellow football. Late in the winter we were blessed with a fresh snowfall and I took Tasha for a walk off lead across the snow, up the hill covered with pine trees, and we played together.

Blanca and Ici stood watching us as we returned to the house. The two huskies stood together, and it struck me as I realized that soon this is how it would be; just Blanca and Ici - together. It was the last walk in the snow my lead dog would ever make.

When her time came I fell asleep next to Tasha on the floor. Tasha at my side snuggled next to me with her warm soft fur pressing against my face. Her breathing was heavy as we went to sleep. I dreaded the next day; Tasha's beautiful and athletic body finally failing, I would call Dr. Wolf and he would come and help her sleep.

I woke up the next day and there the beautiful Tasha was, still snuggled next to me with her soft fur pressed against my face, her chin resting comfortably on her forepaw, and a look of happiness and contentment on her face. After all, Tasha was in her most loved place; she was at my side. Even in passing, she would be no trouble. I sat up and looked at this beautiful and strong sled dog and stroked her beautiful thick fur for a long time remembering all the wonderful experiences, remembering this greatest of friends, my constant companion, and remembering her love for me that just poured from her eyes warming my heart. I held her and sang her song into her ear. I whispered in her ear the words I dreaded saying from the first moment I saw her, "Farewell my Tasha, my Natasha Ko; I will feel so alone without you at my side."

I buried her on her land next to her love. I buried her with her favorite toy; her fur wet with my tears. Blanca and Ici watched me as I lovingly lowered Tasha into her grave. The two huskies each had the same expression on their faces, seemingly lost and without direction, a shocked look of suddenly placed responsibility. The Alpha, their leader, the one they looked to for safety and guidance was gone. I miss her and with the saddest of hearts I long for the sight of her gazing into my eyes. I think of her often every day. My life is so much less without her love.

The Perfect Sled Dog

Blanca was all sled dog. She was mischievous and hilarious. When people came to visit she would talk at them, "rouw row rah rooh." If she could, she would lick you with this big sloppy wet tongue. She especially liked to do this after drinking water to make it extra wet - enjoying the annoyed and disgusted reaction of the recipient. Then she would go back to her water dish and lay there with her snout in the water blowing bubbles. She was a very happy husky and could always find some way to amuse herself.

She loved attention more than any of the other huskies. When I pet her I would often rub her ruff on both sides and Blanca would purr and rest the top of her head between my feet and roll head over heals toward me, flopping right over. She was always a clown. Most of the huskies were not too concerned with other people and their love and attention was always focused on me or the Currumpaw pack. Being the Omega and the nasty fighter that she was, if you started to pet one of the huskies Blanca would come running and push the other husky away from you in an attempt to hog all the attention. Blanca loved everybody and may have been the happiest sled dog that ever lived.

When she was on the trail she was all business. When I ran all five dogs Blanca would run in the swing position which is in the middle of the gang line between the lead and wheel pairs. I would put her in this position because nothing could distract her from staying on the trail; not if any of the other dogs misbehaved, not even when deer were on the trail. She made mushing the full team easier. At home, she would lay in the house spending hours grooming her feet, biting them, pulling her paw off the floor, making sure they were in perfect order for the next mush.

After Tasha passed, Blanca sat by our huskies' graves letting out her long mournful howls, but she stopped spending too much time outside and started staying by me. I gave her lots of extra attention and she took Tasha's place at my side. Blanca began sleeping next to me, huddled next to Ici on my left and I would slip my right hand under her and she would sleep on my hand the rest of the night. Was she taking Tasha's place or was she keeping close so as not to lose any other pack members? This I will never know because I didn't really have the time with learn all that she felt; Blanca fell ill suddenly.

I honored this great sled dog by washing and grooming her feet for her one last time and I buried her with the other three huskies next to her Leto and Brandenburg. I buried her with her favorite bone and the only remaining Currumpaw, Ici - Currumpaw's Ice Dancer, stood and watched me with remembering eyes as I lowered Blanca into her into her grave.

At Heaven's Gate

When I assembled the team in those early years I would think about how great it would be to live with the pack and spend my life with them. Sled dogs will live well over ten years and having the Currumpaws seemed so permanent. Those years past in an instant.

The Chukchi say that at heaven's gates all the sled dogs that ever lived stand together and anyone who did not treat their sled dogs well shall not pass. There, your sled dogs wait for you, and the way you treated your huskies in this life determines your place in heaven. The little dogs have courage not usually seen in our comfortable world and who better could God have chosen to stand guard at His gates?

After burying Blanca I looked up at Ici. Seeing her standing there all alone without her pack I felt great sympathy for her and I cried out to her with all my heart and from the depth of my soul which had been so enlightened and blessed with experience the of living in the presence of the Currumpaws: "Oh poor Ici, your huskies are gone."

I stood there with Ici and I looked up to the heavens where the sled dogs stand at the gates and told my huskies that Blanca was coming.

I told Leto to play king of the mountain with her, and they should remember to bark and taunt each other, dropping on their forearms while standing on their hind legs, one husky charging suddenly towards the other—the other bolting away laughing.

I told Brandenburg that he should go sniff her and give her this look of contentment as he always did, smiling, with is eyes half closed.

I told Tasha to pounce on Blanca the way she always did, with Blanca trying to bolt past her laughing and scooting as they do; Blanca's back legs beginning to overtake her front legs with her butt and tail down; Tasha standing defiantly while Blanca bolted past, finally leaping through the air in a graceful arch, biting Blanca on the back of the neck.

I will try to walk that road to heaven and should I be so blessed as to make it as far as its gates, and see my Tasha and her Currumpaw pack, and all the Chukchi sled dogs as far as the eyes can see, I will desire to go no further and I will stand with Them.

I can borrow, with a heavy heart, an expression from the Texas cowboys who claim that it was a cruel God that made the horse's life shorter than the cowboy's. It was a cruel God that made the huskies' lives shorter than mine.

The Order of the Pack is Strong

The order of the pack is strong and each member has a special and important place. Tasha and Brandenburg the Alpha pair, Leto the Beta, and Blanca the Omega. It was partially that order that made the Currumpaw Siberians what they were.

That order was most apparent when we would return from a mush. Thirsty, the huskies preferred drinking water from their dish in the house. I never fully appreciated this but while writing this book I remembered. I would fill the large water bowl and the most fascinating thing would happen, each and every time.

The huskies would cue up in single file - in the order of the pack. Brandenburg would drink first and then Tasha, Leto, Ici, and finally Blanca. They would stand in line patiently waiting; the huskies would fight to validate the order of the pack - they would also confirm it with these fascinating and polite gestures. Today, when I make dinner I first fill Ici's dish with her favorite food, then I sit and dine, Ici lying on the floor next to me. When I'm finished, she'll walk to her dish and eat her food.

Sometimes I will just sit and relax in our den or read a book. I will look up to find Ici staring at me. Being predators and pack members, staring was something the huskies rarely did.

Staring is not something that pack members do because it creates a challenge with the dog being stared at. Sometimes the huskies, especially Tasha, would stare at me with loving adoration. But Ici would stare at me with this stoic gaze and she would do this often. At these times her stares were not the stares of loving adoration. What does she see? I remembered the night it was forty below zero and Brandenburg wouldn't come into the house. I remembered him standing out in the bitter cold looking off into the land and then staring out the window once he came back in the house. Ici is a spirit dog and I would wonder if my huskies were watching me through Ici's eyes.

As Ici grew older she often would go into the kennel room where I used to keep the huskies when I was away. The kennel room was in a far corner of the house that we would never pass during a day's activities. There was never any reason for either of us to go there. The room was just an empty space filled with ghosts of days past, days that will never return to my home. Afterwards, Ici would look towards the kennel room from some distance, tilting her head back with her nose in the air sniffing. I never knew for certain why she would go there, but when she began sniffing the air from a distance I realized to was to see if one of the huskies had been hiding there all this time or to remember those wonderful days when the pack was together; sleeping there while waiting for me to return home from work.

Other times Ici would ask to be let out shortly after she had already been outside. When the pack was together, this was common because they wanted to go out on the land and play. She would ask me to let her out and she would go up to the special opening that would let her outside and then suddenly stop and stare out at the land. She would put her head down and slowly walk back to me; there was no longer anything out there for her, her huskies and playmates were gone, and she would come back in because she had an important place at my side.

Ici and I walked to the beginning of the huskies' favorite trail; that fast, long, five mile trail. The trail runs straight and is high above the land. The land slopes off from each side of the trail and to its west side is a steep wooded ravine. The trail is absolutely beautiful and I possess the most wonderful memories of the huskies mushing this trail. I look down the long straight trail that seems to come to a point in the distance, and I remember how fast we could travel the distance, the trees moving by, the sound of the runners, the silent sound of running the dogs. Most of all I remembered the exuberance of the team as they waited to start, the joy that came from the team as we sped along the trail, and their fulfillment as they did this thing they thought was so necessary to me.

I worry for Ici. When she looks around her land she does not see the comforting sight of her pack, of her kind. She is the last of the Currumpaws.

Of Dr. Bruce Wolf; the Absent Pack Member

I entered into the experience of raising the Currumpaws with a great deal of knowledge of dog training and knowledge of huskies and dog sledding. I also have a great deal of knowledge caring for the health of the dogs, but it is little when compared to that of a veterinarian.

On the far opposite side of the city is a veterinary practice owned and led by Dr. Wolf. He is a gentle man with sparkling eyes who loves people and animals alike. Dr. Wolf possesses qualities that are mostly absent in today's world. His is extremely generous and possesses a thirst for knowledge to further his skills and abilities. Everything Dr. Wolf did was compassionate and generous and surely this kindness was returned to him daily because, as they say, there is no gift like giving. It was very inconvenient for me to drive to and across the city to see him, but his talents were not likely to be replicated anywhere else so he became the caretaker of the Currmupaw pack's health.

Dr. Wolf treated many types of animals and specialized in caring for Rottweillers, but when he realized that he had the chance to care for and learn from the Currumpaws, what he called "real working dogs", he stepped up to the challenge and opportunity with great enthusiasm. How ironic I thought, almost funny, to find a doctor with the name "Wolf" to care for the Currumpaws.

Dr. Wolf completely gave of himself to the Currumpaws. No one could have provided better care, more intelligent analysis and diagnosis, or more kindness to the pack. Sometimes I would have to leave one of the huskies over night at the clinic and he would "borrow" that husky from the clinic and take it home with him to both observe and enjoy. I'm glad he did this because despite all his time and effort he did not experience the overwhelming amount of joy that I received from living my life with the pack. At least by taking them to his home during their times of sickness he was able to share a little bit of the joy of the Currumpaws. He always felt their pain and their hard times and later cried upon each one of their deaths as if they were his own huskies.

Evening

Its evening and I will relax as I always do, with Ici lying in her favorite spot, next to the sled with which they upset the mushing world. She stretches out, with her head touching the runners of her sled, falling asleep. While asleep, her legs will twitch and she'll make little yelps. I wish I could be in her dream with her as she surely must be running with a sled and her Currumpaw pack tugging on the neckline that attached her to Tasha, when Ici got the left command "haw". I know she's dreaming of playing with her beloved Leto and of seeing all the Currumpaw sled dogs, her family, and her pack.

It's a beautiful morning and Ici will wake up from sleeping on my left, next to the space at the corner of the bed where her beloved Leto slept. In this way she takes Leto's place – remembering - as is the way of the pack. I miss the days when Ici slept over my right leg and I would wake feeling her head resting on my thigh. This was her place when the pack was intact. No matter how much time I spent with the pack, regardless of how well I came to understand the ways of the pack, being human I still long for the days when Ici slept over my right leg.

With Leto and the rest of the pack gone, my stoic little Ici must take their place, and take the place of the missing Alpha, my Tasha. The lower pack members, including Leto, could enjoy a pleasure that Tasha never could, because this was a pleasure that was not for their leader. The huskies would often huddle together when they rested and napped. They huddled in the most endearing ways, snuggled up together keeping each other warm, even in the summer. When Ici was a pack member she would sleep over my right leg every night. Now she is the Alpha and she sleeps at my left, without the comfort of the huddle, because as the Alpha, she must maintain that stoic aloofness that is the posture of the strongest, the leader. I wish it were not this way but with this change Ici fulfills her life, the life of a pack-member.

It's Sunday and Ici will have fun. Ici rides in my truck, standing behind me with her head sticking slightly out the window, occasionally touching her nose to my cheek. I look over at her and I can see the splendor of what she is, standing proudly, carrying the experiences of living with her pack, the love she gave and the love she received. She stands proud as no common animal ever could, with a little piece of each of the Currumpaws living in her heart, glowing from her pride and the wonder of her life experience, knowing that she has lived the way God intended her to - serving the People and living with the Pack; true to her being, true to all that the sled dogs ever were and all that the sled dog is.

Unlike the Siberian Huskies we often see proudly walking with their owners and riding in their cars, Ici stands with a special pride, and has a light that just glows from her eyes - Ici is a sled dog. Ici is a lead dog and like the rest of the Currumpaws, followed the only good trail in life there is to follow.

Ici gets to do all kinds of things she couldn't do in the past, when there were too many dogs to take with me everywhere. She will go to my family's house for a family dinner and get treats and she'll have lots of fun, after all, fun is what a sled dog's life is about. She will go to sleep happy, with her sleeping partner, snuggled up on his left, somehow knowing that the Chukchis, my totem - the wolf spirit, and all the Chukchi sled dogs at the gates of heaven are smiling on her.

Ici is well and will likely live long so as not to disturb the strong order of the pack because, you see, she is not the last of the Currumpaws—to her there are still two of us and she won't want to leave me alone.

The Survival of the Pack

The survival of the pack is a strong instinct and the story of the Currumpaws lives on through Ici. Ici adds to my joy of living with them and my experience of being blessed with the company and love of the sled dog. But things change and now Ici does not always wake on my left, nor does she wake on my right as she did for most of the days of her life. Ici has a gift of empathy and she can feel what people feel, and most of all she can feel what I feel.

There are certain times, in certain situations that Ici wakes elsewhere - in a special place where she waits for assurance that her pack will live on. It is the fault of my own heart that she does this and I do not like these times when she does not wake at my side. I will let Ici live out the rest of her days with this hope she demonstrates by where she sometimes wakes. But unlike the story of the Currumpaws, this is a story of her heartbreak and Ici's hope and because of my love for her its one that I can never tell.

I will let Ici have her hope and I will learn from her as I have lived to feel the mettle of the Chukchi Sled Dog. I am blessed to know that their strengths really do exist in this world. We should all learn from them; loyalty, unconditional love, joy and love for life and the Earth, to never quit, never give up hope, and show the traits as engraved on the statue of Balto in Central Park. I promise Ici that I will have hope as well and, God willing, that her hopes might be realized in the many ways she needs.

Another Currumpaw Morning

The sun is rising and I wake as the light beams through the window and shines on Ici. I and feel her warm furry presence to my left. She's still sleeping. She's had a wondrous life and has been going to sleep even happier these days because perhaps her hopes and dreams have finally been realized - Ici's hope that her pack will live on. I get closer to my Pretty and put my arms around her, holding her tight, feeling her soft fur, and smelling the wonderful clean fur smell that huskies have. I lay with her and hold her for a long while because this day, I don't want to get out of bed either.

I walk downstairs to my big family room and just lay on the couch for a while - remembering my huskies and the endless joyful days of living with the Currumpaws. I remembered their playful antics, their passion for the mush, their love for each other and the love they had for me. I thought of all our wonderful experiences on the trail, their courage, and their stunning strength and beauty.

The family room is decorated with artifacts reflecting the sled dog breeding cultures of the American Eskimo and the Chukchi and with many wonderful things collected or won during our years of dog sledding. It's not a family room. It's the den of the Currumpaws. This is where they spent their time while in the house. One of Tasha's little yellow footballs still sits on the window sill. Pictures of the Currumpaws are everywhere, capturing their puppy-hood, their personalities, and the energy and joyous enthusiasm of the mush. There are two picture albums beautifully bound in rich walnut sitting on the wet-bar; chronologies of the pack's lives from their births to their glorious days on the trail. There are even pictures of Tasha's last walk in the snow and the haunting pictures of Ici and Blanca standing alone together waiting for our return.

This room is also where the Currumpaws' racing sled rests, forever still without its team. Lying in the sled's basket are the retired harnesses and sled dog collars of my huskies. The neon colored harnesses are laid out next to each other, still glowing with the energy of the dogs that once so proudly wore them. I walk over to where I keep my sled dog equipment and get Ici's harness and collar and lay them down on the sled with the others. Now my sled is complete.

I walk outside and spend some time doing today's necessary work, then return to the house to get my precious Pretty. Ici and I go outside on the huskies' land and we walk to where my huskies are sleeping in the earth.

I put my hand on each of the large sandstones that mark each one of my husky's resting spots and ask them each something different. I ask Brandenburg to help teach me patience and contentment, I ask Leto to continue to protect me and teach me courage, I ask Blanca to help teach me joy and I ask Tasha to help show me the way that I may always choose the only good trail in life there is to follow.

We walk to the spot right next to where Ici's beloved Leto lays. I look over to my left to the empty space on the huskies' land that was once filled with the joy, hilarious antics, and life of the Currumpaw pack. There are no huskies watching me as I tremble while gently lowering my dearest Ici, my Pretty, into her grave.

Now Ici and Leto are sleeping side by side once again and my huskies are sleeping flanked by my two great lead dogs. All my huskies are together again. My land lies where my dead lay buried[4]; I pray I never to leave this land that is theirs.

There is a mushers' legend that says your huskies lay sleeping waiting for you, and when you come across, they greet you with all that joy the accompanied every meeting and the beginning of every mush. All together again, they pull your sled through and into heaven. I miss my life with the Currumpaws, and I miss each of them. It will not be possible for me to raise a pack the way the Currumpaws were raised and I will never again feel the love that poured from each of their eyes, the love that grew in these little beings that could only come from their experience of being raised as a pack and living their lives as sled dogs. The Currumpaw pack lives on in my heart. From where the sun now stands, I will mush no more forever[5].

I will try to walk that road to heaven and live my life as God intended me to so that I should be so blessed that one day the Currumpaws will awake and we will be reunited. Tasha and her pack will pull my sled on that final journey.

I look up to heaven where the Chukchi dogs stand at its gates and imagine Ici arriving and seeing all my huskies joyfully running up to her with their noses touching and tails wagging as is the way of the pack's greeting. Suddenly all the Chukchi sled dogs turn and look toward the gates, smiling, as huskies do. Someone is peering through the gates and He looks through the gates toward His huskies, which stand as far as the eyes can see and smiles back knowing that once again, He did Good. A good lead dog always brings the team home.

Trail Ends

.

Acknowledgements & References

[1] **Currumpaw; The Story of the Currumpaw Wolf: Outlaw Wolves** – From "Of Wolves and Men", By Barry Lopez

"One of the more poignant stories about an outlaw or renegade wolf concerns that Currumpaw Wolf of northern New Mexico and his mate Blanca, who were killed in 1894 by the naturalist Ernest Thompson Seton.

Seton, called in by a concerned rancher who was a friend, tried every sort of set he could devise, to no avail. Each time, the Currumpaw Wolf would dig up and spring the traps or pointedly ignore them.

One evening Seton set out to concoct the be-all-and-end-all of baits: "Acting on the hint of an old trapper, I melted some cheese together with the kidney fat of a freshly killed heifer, stewing it in a china dish, and cutting it with a bone knife to avoid the taint of metal. When the mixture was cool, I cut it into lumps, and making a hole in the side of each lump I inserted a large dose of strychnine and cyanide, contained in a capsule that was impermeable by any odor; finally I sealed the holes with pieces of the cheese itself. During the whole process, I wore a pair of gloves, steeped in the hot blood of the heifer, and even avoided breathing on the baits. When all was ready, I put them in a raw-hide bag rubbed all over with blood, and rode forth dragging the liver and kidneys of the beef at the end of a rope. With this I made a ten mile circuit, dropping a bait at each quarter mile, and taking the utmost care, always not to touch any with my hands."

Seton's caution and arcane science were techniques much praised by wolfers of the time. The Currumpaw Wolf, for his part, carefully gathered four of the baits in a pile and defecated on them.

The female wolf, Blanca, was finally caught in a steel trap in the spring of 1894. Seton and a companion approached the wolf on horseback. "Then followed the inevitable tragedy, the idea of which I shrank from afterward more than at the time. We threw a lasso over the neck of the doomed wolf, and strained our horses in opposite directions until the blood burst from her mouth, her eyes glazed, her limbs stiffened and then fell limp."

The dead female was taken back to the ranch. The male, abandoning all his former caution, followed her and the next day stepped into a nest of traps set around the ranch buildings. He was chained up and left for the night but was found dead in the morning, without a wound or any sign of a struggle. Seton, deeply moved by what happened, placed his dead body in the shed next to Blanca's.

The price offered to the man who would kill the Currumpaw Wolf was one thousand dollars. Seton never says whether he took it."

In hindsight we know that it was not just the Currumpaw Wolf that dug up the traps and made insult of the poisons left for his pack—it was the Alpha pair, the Wolf and his mate Blanca. The Alpha male brings strength and confidence to the pack, but it was the intelligence, and vigilant passion and concern for the well being of the pack that came from the Alpha female that caused many of the events that saved the Currumpaw Wolf's pack.

The order of the pack is strong each member having its own special and important place. Wolf packs grow to a certain size, a size that is dictated by the resources of their territory. Each member has an important place in the hunt, and the pack cannot support the weak, the sick, or the very old. Somehow wolves communicate a strategy that is played out during the hunt—it is not known how such abstract concepts are communicated among wolves.

Knowing this, there is a lesson for us all. In the late nineteen eighties a wolf biologist observed a pack that included a very old female. Somewhat healthy, the old female had no teeth—broken from years of hunting and deteriorated from age. Teeth are critical to a successful hunt. By watching this pack the biologist realized that she too possessed something crucial to the survival of the pack and the success of the hunt—she possessed knowledge.

****

[2] After the serum run, Seppala toured North America with Togo and many of his sled dogs. They ran in many races, winning most of them. Togo retired to the farm of Mrs. Elizabeth Ricker, who was instrumental in bringing the breed to its present state of popularity. Togo spent the rest of his life in her wonderful surroundings, and she paid special attention to him. Togo died on December 5, 1929.

[3] The Amish refer to non-Amish cultures as "the English".

[4] My land lies where my dead lay buried.

This phrase is taken from the words of Crazy Horse, the Sioux warrior. Upon the final defeat of the Indian Nation in 1877, the remaining warriors were taken to a fort to wait to be moved to a reservation. For all the courage and heartbreak of the native Americans, the soldiers mocked the warriors, who were now heartbroken and forcibly removed from their place in God's plan, the Earth. One soldier recognized Crazy Horse, laughing he said, "Where's your land now Crazy Horse?" Crazy Horse turned, extended his arm and point out to the Land saying, "My land lies where my dead lay buried".

****

⁵ **From where the sun now stands I will mush no more forever.**

> This phrase is taken from the words of Chief Joseph, named Hinmaton Kalakitt of the Nez Perce tribe. Defeated, broken hearted, and removed from their place in God's Land following the great slaughter at Wounded Knee in 1877, the chief surrendered to the American Army on behalf of the native people—speaking not to the conquering American colonel and his officers, but directly to the chiefs of the remaining People:

"I am tired of fighting. Our chiefs are killed. Looking Glass is dead. Toohulhulsote is dead. The old men are all dead. It is the young men who say no and yes. He who led the young men is dead.

It is cold and we have no blankets. The little children are freezing to death.

My people, some of them, have run away to the hills and have no blankets, no food.

No one knows where they are—perhaps they are freezing to death.

I want to have time to look for my children and see how many of them I can find.

Maybe I shall find them among the dead.

Hear me, my chiefs, I am tired. My heart is sad and sick.

From where the sun now stands I will fight no more forever."

The Trail Continues

My brother Denny was unable to publish his book is because on April 30th, 2004 he was killed in a motorcycle accident. During Easter he was talking about having a book signing once it was published. He was so happy how it turned out and all the great feedback he received from family & friends the read his manuscript. I was fortunate to spend quality time with him during Easter. We never know when the angel of death is going to come for us. He took care of the pack as they fell ill kept them comfortable until death. Riding his Harley was his preferred transportation so he died doing what he loved. Denny for as long as I can remember liked to be in the wind whether it was driving in the winter with the windows down, Skiing, Cycling or riding motorcycles. He has now reunited with the huskies at heavens gate. Now together again Denny is on his sled with Tasha Ko leading the pack to heavens journey.

Denny with sister Debbie

About the Author

By Al & Grace Abarca

- At 7 years old he played a duet recital for the Hammond Society.
- High school he was with the National Ski Patrol @ Brandywine.
- Ohio Region 1975-1976 Ski & Toboggan Competition:
- First Place – Hot Dog Event
- He went on to win many other competitions which led him to ski with US Ski Team
- Started Rainbow Freestyle Productions
- Built a mobile carpeted treadmill powered by 3 hp, 20V motor ski deck.
- Exhibition of freestyle skiing @ Dayton Ski & Winter Sports fair, many malls
- "Winter Dreams Deck Show" @ Cleveland Ski & Winter Sports Fair
- Built a slide at a Lake in Lodi, Ohio to practice Flipping on skis landing in water
- Started team Equipe Velo Club member of the U.S. Cycling Federation

- Massillon Bicycle Race Licensed 25 miles 18 & over 3 rd Place
- Grand Prix of Cycling Toronto, Canada

The Following Denny won many Ribbons & Metals:

- 1982 The Wildwoods USA Pro AM Bike Race
- 1982 U.S. Cycling Federation District Championship Sr. Men Pursuit
- 1983 U.S. Cycling Federation District Championship Sr. Men Kilo
- 1983 U.S. Cycling Federation District Championship Sr. Men
- 1983 U.S. Cycling Federation Sr. men Sprints

- 1984 Lehigh County Velodrome USCF
- 1984 U.S. Cycling Federation District Championship Sr. Men Pt. Race
- 1984 U.S. Cycling Federation District Championship Sr. Men Sprints
- 1985 U.S. Cycling federation District Ohio, W. Va., Sr. men Kilo
- 1986 Almost May Day 1st Place Experienced Bike Race
- 1986 Almost May Day 2nd Place 24 – 29 Bike races
- World Masters "Coupe Du Monde" track Championship Minneapolis & St. Johann, Austria
- 1989 Ohio Festival State Games
- 1991 Ohio Festival State Games
- 1991 Eden Soy. Saline Bike Criterium-Masters Category 6th Place
- 1992 REVCO Cleveland Criterium
- 1994 Velodrome NSL World Cup
- 1994 Medina YWCA Twin Sizzler Expert Bike Race 1st Place

Siberian Husky Club of Greater Cleveland

- Four Ribbons – First, Second & Third Place
- Buckeye Feeds Classic 3 Dog Sled Pure Bred 1st place & 2 Trophies
- 1st Place weight Pull
- Buckeye Feeds Classic Fastest All Siberian Team 3 Dog Class 4 Trophies
- Siberian Husky Club 3rd Fastest 4 Dog Team

Articles Published

- Pollution Engineering October 1998
"Implementing ISO 9000 & ISO 14000 By: Dennis Abarca
- Quality Digest February 1999
"Making the Most of Internal Audits" By: Dennis Abarca
- Environmental Protection November 1998
"A Platform for Pollution Prevention by: Dennis Abarca

CPSIA information can be obtained
at www.ICGtesting.com
Printed in the USA
FSOW01n0258250317
32245FS